THE CRÊPE BOOK

By Susan Herbert

Illustrated by Dennis Redmond

Editor: Susan Herbert
Home Economist: Karen Plageman

2

TABLE OF CONTENTS

Dennis Redmond

INTRODUCTION

The whole world loves crêpes. And no wonder! These elegant little pancakes wrap up so many national dishes. France, of course, has its renowned suzette. Russia has blinchikas; Hungary has palascintas. There are Jewish blintzes of delectable variety and a grand version of Italian cannelloni. All start with easy-to-do crêpes.

But this is just the beginning of the countless ways you will serve crêpes. You can take leftover turkey or ham and turn out a proud entrée. Or make a vegetable crêpe that's truly memorable. And you'll whip up desserts that will delight everyone in the house. There are crêpes for breakfast, lunch and dinner! All are fun, quite simple to do—and the best part is you can make everything ahead of time and heat it up at the last minute.

There are three steps to most crêpe dishes: the crêpes, the filling, and, usually, a sauce that covers all. Although there is a technique to making crêpes, once you have mastered it you'll make crêpes as easily as pancakes. The batter itself is simple—but you do need a special crêpe pan.

THE CRÊPE PAN IS ESSENTIAL! Thanks to today's ingenuity there are two ways to cook your crêpes. You may use the conventional crêpe pan; pour a little batter in and cook the crêpe pancake-style. Or you may use one of the new "upside-down" crêpe pans; dip the pan in the batter and cook the crêpe on the bottom of the pan.

If you are going to make crêpes in the conventional manner, start with a small skillet or frying pan that measures about 6 to 8 inches across the bottom. The pan should be of heavy cast iron, aluminum or steel. And it must be properly seasoned according to its particular instructions. (Once a pan has been seasoned for crêpes—never use it for anything but crêpe-making.)

Heat the crêpe pan and brush it lightly with butter, margarine or oil. Let it heat until just about smoking. Pour in 2 or 3 tablespoons of batter (a gravy ladle is a perfect measure.) Quickly tilt the pan in all directions to cover the bottom surface with a very thin layer of batter. Cook the crêpe over a medium high heat until the underside is browned. This should take about a minute. Then turn the crêpe with a spatula or carefully with your fingers and brown the other side for about 30 seconds. (The second side is spotty and is used as the "inside.") Place the crêpe browned side up on a plate. Grease the crêpe pan again as necessary and repeat the steps to make the rest of the crêpes. Use the crêpes right away or cover with plastic wrap and refrigerate until needed. (See storing instructions.)

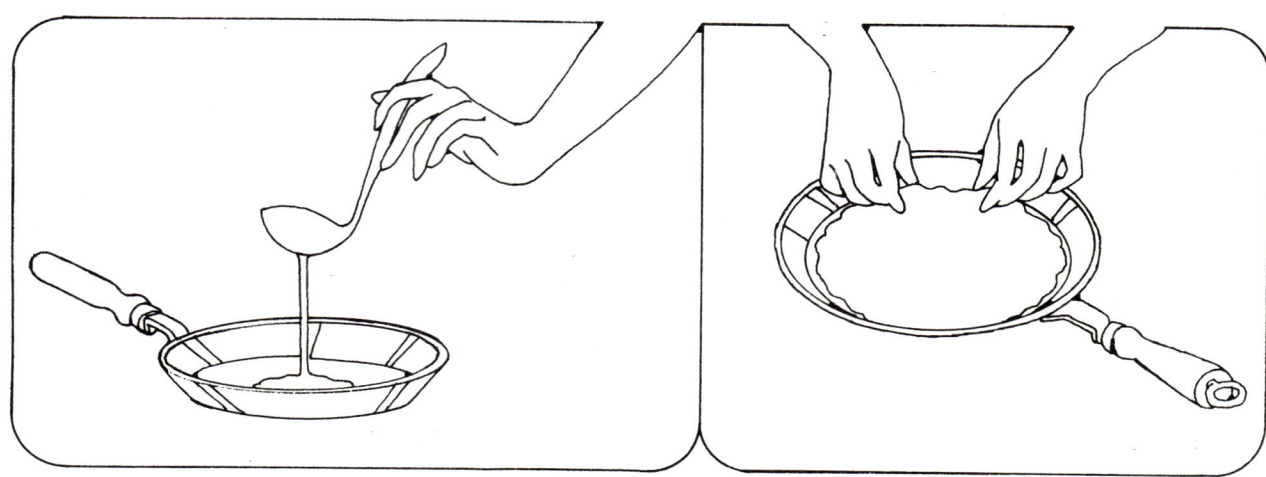

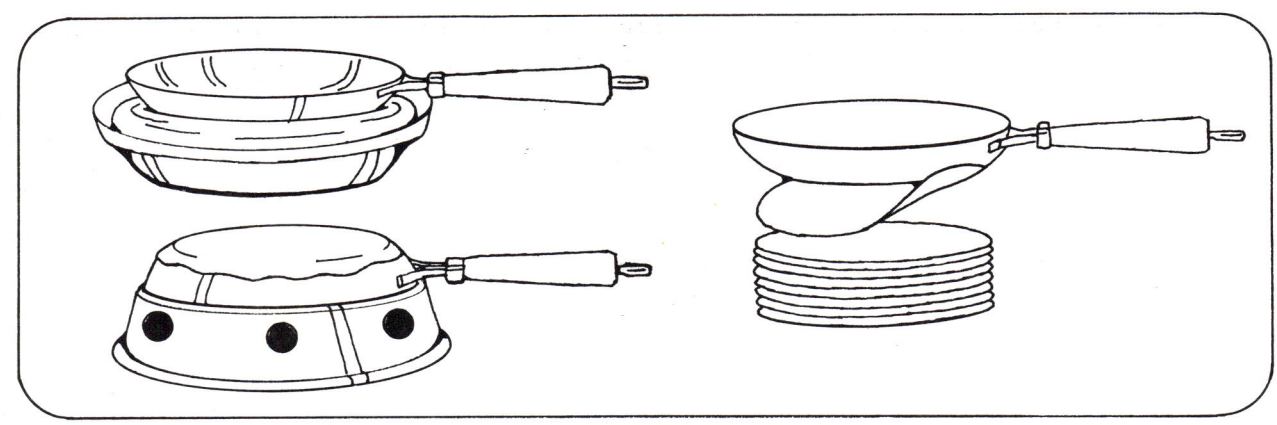

If you plan to make crêpes with an "upside-down" crêpe pan, follow these easy steps. Be sure pan is seasoned as instructed. Pour the prepared batter into a shallow dish or pie pan. Preheat crêpe pan over a medium-high heat and test for readiness. (When a small piece of butter melts and bubbles on the pan the temperature is correct.) Dip the crêpe pan into the batter in an even motion to obtain an even coating. Turn the pan over and cook until the edges begin to turn a golden brown. (Patch the crêpes if necessary with a drop or two of batter.) This will take about 45 seconds. Invert the pan and let the crêpe come off onto a plate. Sometimes you may have to loosen the crêpe edges a bit with a table knife.

To remove any crumbs, wipe the pan lightly with an oil-moistened paper towel. Repeat the procedure and make the rest of the crêpes. If the batter does not adhere to the pan and a skim of cooked batter floats on the batter mix, the pan is too hot. Remove the skim and adjust heat.

START WITH THE CRÊPES

Here are a variety of crêpe batters from which to choose. There are two basic types: a batter for entrée dishes and a sweeter batter for dessert crêpes. Some recipes suggest a particular crêpe batter, others do not. But with all the recipes you should feel free to try different crêpe batters. You'll soon discover your favorites and create crêpe dishes with a personal flair.

BASIC ENTRÉE CRÊPES
use this for any entrée selection

1 cup all-purpose flour, sifted or presifted
3/4 cup water
3/4 cup milk
3 eggs
2 tablespoons melted butter or margarine, cooled
1/4 teaspoon salt

Use blender, mixer or wire whisk as directed on page 13. Makes 14 to 16 crêpes.

8

WHOLEWHEAT CRÊPES
delicious crêpes with a wholesome texture

1 cup whole wheat flour
1-1/2 cups milk
3 eggs
2 tablespoons melted butter or margarine, cooled
1/4 teaspoon salt

Use blender, mixer or wire whick as directed on page 13. Makes 14 to 16 crêpes.

CRÊPES WITH HERBS
perfect wrap-up for an herbed filling

1 cup all-purpose flour, sifted or presifted
3/4 cup water
3/4 cup milk
3 eggs
2 tablespoons melted butter or margarine, cooled
1/4 teaspoon salt
2 tablespoons minced dill, chives or parsley

Use blender, mixer or wire whisk as directed on page 13. Makes 14 to 16 crêpes.

BEER CRÊPES
perfect with hearty meat fillings

1-1/2 cups all-purpose flour, sifted or presifted
11 or 12 oz. can of beer
3 eggs
2 tablespoons melted butter or margarine, cooled
1/4 teaspoon salt

Use blender, mixer or wire whisk as directed on page 13. Makes 16 to 20 crêpes.

BASIC DESSERT CRÊPES
sweet and light with a hint of spirits

1-1/2 cups all-purpose flour, sifted or presifted
3/4 cup milk
3/4 cup cold water
2 whole eggs
2 egg yolks

1/4 cup melted butter or margarine, cooled
2 tablespoons sugar
1/8 teaspoon salt
3 tablespoons brandy, rum or liqueur

Use blender, mixer or wire whisk as directed on page 13. Makes 24 to 26 crêpes.

YEAST DESSERT CRÊPES
a tender crêpe that's just a bit thicker

3/4 cup milk

1 package dry or compressed yeast

3/4 cup water

2 whole eggs

2 egg yolks

2 tablespoons sugar

1/8 teaspoon salt

3 tablespoons cognac or brandy

1-1/2 cups all-purpose flour, sifted or presifted

1/4 cup melted butter or margarine, cooled

Warm 1/4 cup of milk to lukewarm if using compressed yeast or to very warm if using dry yeast. Sprinkle yeast into milk. Let stand a few minutes, then stir until yeast is dissolved. Add this to rest of ingredients and mix with blender, mixer or wire whisk as directed on page 13. Cover batter with a towel and let stand at room temperature for 2 hours or until batter looks bubbly. Use immediately or yeast will overferment. Makes 24 to 28 crêpes.

PUFFY DESSERT CRÊPES
beaten egg whites make a "raised" crêpe

Make yeast crêpe batter. After batter has stood at room temperature for two hours and immediately before you plan to make crêpes, beat 2 egg whites with 1/8 teaspoon salt until stiff. Gently fold into batter and make crêpes. Makes 24 to 28 crêpes.

ORANGE HONEY CRÊPES
try these with fresh fruit fillings

1 cup all-purpose flour, sifted or presifted
1 cup sour cream
1/2 cup milk
1/2 cup orange juice
2 eggs
2 tablespoons sugar
1 teaspoon salt
2 teaspoons grated orange peel

Use blender, mixer or wire whisk as directed on page 13. Makes 16 to 18 crêpes.

SOUR CREAM CRÊPES
use for blintzes and some desserts

1 cup all-purpose flour, sifted or presifted
2 eggs
2/3 cup milk
2/3 cup sour cream
1/4 teaspoon salt

Use blender, mixer or wire whisk as directed on page 13.
Makes 14 to 16 crêpes.

12

MAKING THE CRÊPES

There are three easy ways to mix crêpes. Choose the method that is most convenient for you.

THE BLENDER WAY Put all ingredients in a blender jar and whirl for about 1 minute at high speed. Scrape down sides with a spatula and whirl again at high speed for another 15 seconds. Pour into bowl and cover. Refrigerate for an hour or more.

USING A MIXER Beat eggs well. Add the other ingredients and mix with a hand or electric mixer until smooth. Cover and refrigerate for an hour or more.

USING A WIRE WHISK Gradually blend the eggs into the flour, whisk in liquid by spoonsful, then the butter. Strain the batter to remove any lumps. Cover and refrigerate for an hour or more.

With all the batters and methods of mixing, the batter should be allowed to rest for an hour or more (a couple of days if you wish). This enables the flour to expand and assures a light, thin crêpe. If any foam appears, gently stir down or allow the batter to rest a little longer.

THE PROPER CONSISTENCY When you are ready to cook the crêpes, test the batter for the right consistency. If it has separated stir it gently. It should be as thick as heavy cream. If too thin carefully whisk in a tablespoon or so of flour. If too thick, beat in a few teaspoons of water. Consistency will vary with ingredients. Large eggs and homogenized milk should be used. Non-fat milk can be substituted but batter will require additional flour.

REMEMBER YOUR FIRST CRÊPE IS A TEST CRÊPE This is the time to judge batter consistency as well as pan temperature and to make any adjustments.

HOW TO FOLD AND SERVE THE CRÊPES

Just as crêpes can be filled and sauced in so many surprising ways, they can also be folded and shaped with great variety.

CRÊPES CAN BE FOLDED Place the filling along the center of the crêpe browned-side down. Fold one side over the filling, then fold the other side over. Bake and serve seam-side up.

MAKE CRÊPE POCKETS Perfect for blintzes or deep fried crêpes. Place crêpe browned-side up on plate and place filling in center. Fold over opposite sides, then both ends to cover filling completely. Bake and serve with flap-side down.

YOU CAN ROLL UP CRÊPES Place crêpe browned-side down and spoon filling onto the lower third of crêpe. Roll into a cylinder and place seam-side down to bake and serve.

MAKE WEDGES OR TRIANGLES Ideal for crêpes served with just a sauce. Fold crêpes in half, then in half again for a quartered effect. If filled, these wedges give a cornucopia effect.

STACK THE CRÊPES IN A MOUND Center a crêpe browned-side up on a plate and spread with a thin layer of filling. Press another crêpe on top and repeat filling. Continue stacking as recipe indicates. Cut in pie-fashion to serve.

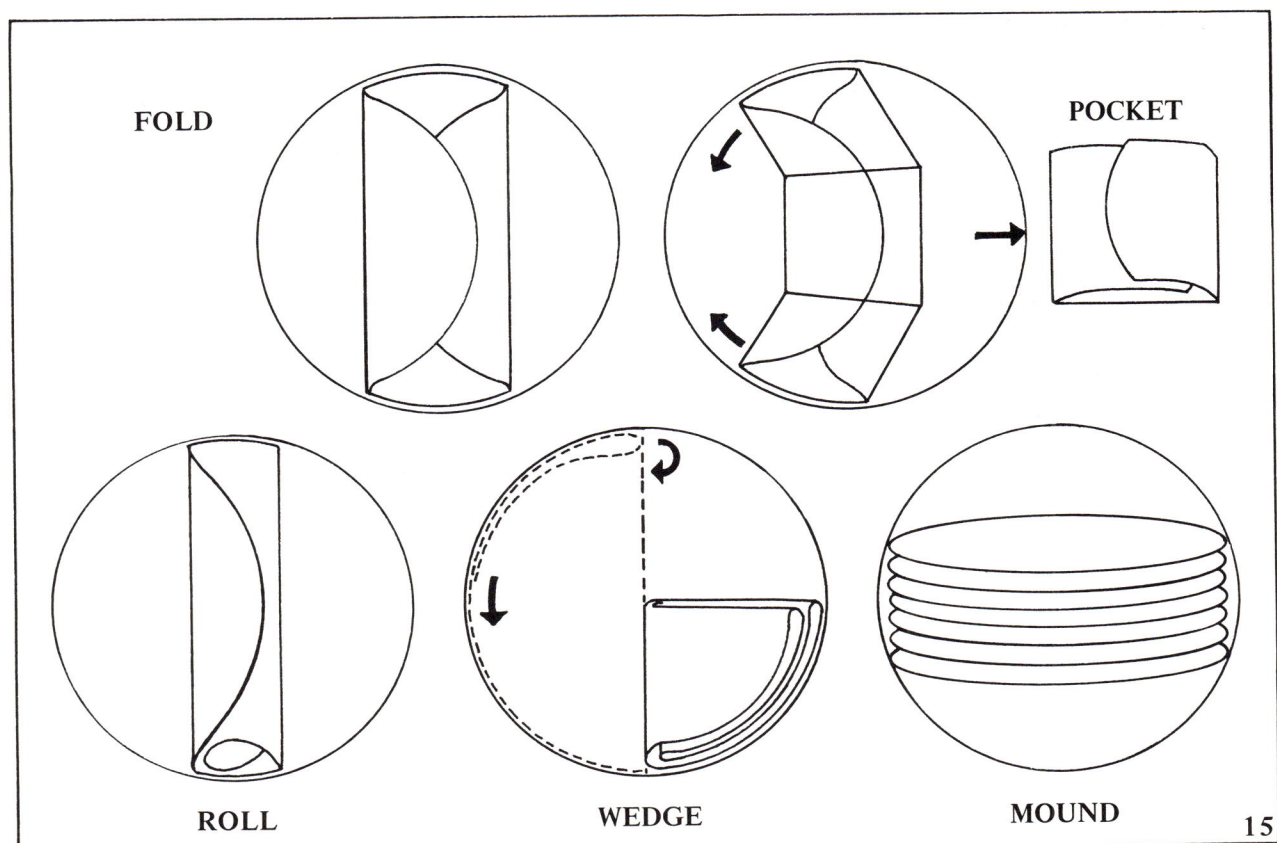

FOLD

POCKET

ROLL

WEDGE

MOUND

15

MAKE CRÊPES NOW AND SERVE THEM LATER

You can make the batter, the crêpes or the filled crêpes ahead of time and finish up at your convenience or at the last minute. The timing is easy and flexible.

Crêpe batter can be stored covered in the refrigerator for several hours or several days. Before using, adjust to a heavy cream consistency with flour or liquid if necessary.

Cooked crêpes can be stacked and wrapped securely with plastic wrap and kept in the refrigerator for several days—or in the freezer for several weeks. Let the crêpes come to room temperature and they will separate easily.

You can even freeze filled crêpes and be ready for guests anytime. After filling the crêpes, place them about 2 inches apart on a cookie sheet and put in freezer. When frozen, remove and, after tightly wrapping each individual crêpe in freezer wrap, return to freezer.

HOW MANY CRÊPES PER PERSON?   This, of course, will vary. As a rule of thumb, count on two or three entrée crêpes per person. When serving dessert crêpes, allow two filled crêpes, or three or more unfilled, sauced crêpes per person.

MAKE A MEMORABLE ENTRÉE

CHICKEN AND ARTICHOKE CRÊPES
a delicious counterplay of flavors

16 entrée crêpes
5 tablespoons butter or margarine
1/2 cup minced onion
1/4 lb. mushrooms, sliced
3 tablespoons all-purpose flour
2/3 cup chicken broth
1/2 cup light cream

2-1/2 cups diced cooked chicken or turkey
1 (10-oz.) package frozen artichoke hearts,
   thawed, drained and cut into fourths
1/3 cup grated Parmesan cheese
1/2 teaspoon crushed rosemary
1/2 teaspoon salt
3/4 cup shredded Swiss cheese

Melt 2 tablespoons butter or margarine in skillet; add onion and mushrooms. Cook, stirring, until mushrooms are limp. Stir in remaining butter or margarine until melted; add flour and cook until bubbly. Gradually stir in broth and cream. Cook, stirring, until sauce boils and thickens. Remove from heat. Stir in chicken, artichokes, Parmesan cheese, rosemary and salt. Divide evenly among crêpes. Roll up and place in single layer in greased shallow baking dish. Dish can be covered and refrigerated at this point. Before serving bake, uncovered, in 350° oven for 15 to 20 minutes or until hot. Sprinkle with Swiss cheese and continue baking 5 minutes or until cheese melts.

CHICKEN CRÊPES WITH AVOCADO
family and guests will rave about these

8 entrée crêpes
5 tablespoons butter or margarine
5 tablespoons flour
1 cup heavy cream
1 cup chicken broth
3/4 cup dry white wine
1 cup grated Swiss cheese
1/2 teaspoon Worcestershire sauce

1 teaspoon salt
1/4 teaspoon pepper
2 tablespoons chopped parsley
2 cups diced, cooked chicken
1/2 cup ripe olive slices
avocado slices
paprika

Melt butter or margarine in saucepan and stir in flour. Add cream, broth and wine. Cook, stirring constantly, until mixture is thickened and smooth. Add 3/4 cup of the cheese and stir until melted. Add Worcestershire sauce, salt, pepper and parsley. Add one cup of this sauce to combined chicken and olives. Divide mixture evenly among crêpes and roll up. Place in single layer in greased shallow baking dish. Dish can be covered and refrigerated at this point. Refrigerate sauce, too. Before serving top each crêpe with an avocado slice and pour remaining sauce, warmed, over all. Sprinkle with remaining cheese and dust with paprika. Bake uncovered in 375° oven for 15 to 20 minutes or until hot, bubbly and lightly browned.

CHICKEN AND HAM CRÊPES
elegant crêpes from holiday leftovers

12 entrée crêpes
1-1/2 cups diced chicken
1 cup diced cooked ham
1 cup frozen peas, partially thawed
1/4 cup butter or margarine
1/2 cup flour
2 cups chicken broth
1/4 cup Madiera or sherry

1 egg yolk
1/3 cup light cream
1/4 cup grated Parmesan cheese
1/2 teaspoon salt
1/4 teaspoon white pepper
3 tablespoons grated Parmesan cheese
3 tablespoons butter or margarine

Mix chicken and ham with peas; set aside. To make sauce, melt 1/4 cup butter or margarine in a saucepan, stir in flour and cook over low heat for 2 minutes, stirring constantly. Remove pan from heat and add broth. Stir until smooth. Add Madiera or sherry and boil gently for 8 minutes. Add egg yolk, lightly beaten with cream and Parmesan cheese. Stir until cheese is melted but do not boil. Remove from heat. Add 1 cup of the sauce to the chicken, ham and peas. Season with salt and pepper. Divide mixture evenly among crêpes, roll up and place in single layer in greased shallow baking dish. Pour remaining sauce over crêpes and sprinkle with 3 tablespoons Parmesan cheese and dot with 3 tablespoons butter or margarine. Dish can be covered and refrigerated at this point. Before serving heat in 375° oven, uncovered, for 15 to 20 minutes or until hot and lightly browned.

CHICKEN LIVER CRÊPES
a favorite variety meat with a great sauce

16 entrée crêpes
1 lb. chicken livers
1/2 cup plus 2 tablespoons butter or margarine
1/3 cup finely chopped green onions
1/2 lb. fresh mushrooms, chopped
1 tablespoon parsley flakes
1 teaspoon poultry seasoning

1/4 cup all-purpose flour
2 cups chicken broth
1 cup light cream
1 teaspoon salt
1/4 teaspoon pepper
1 teaspoon lemon juice
1 cup grated Swiss cheese

Flour chicken livers and sauté in 1/4 cup butter or margarine in skillet. Dice and set aside. Sauté onions and mushrooms in 2 tablespoons butter or margarine until limp. Stir in parsley and poultry seasoning; set aside. In saucepan melt 1/4 cup butter or margarine. Add flour and cook stirring constantly until bubbly. Gradually stir in broth and cream. Cook, stirring, until it boils and thickens. Remove from heat and mix in salt, pepper, and lemon juice. Combine chicken livers, mushroom mixture and 3/4 cup of the sauce, mixing well. Divide filling evenly among crêpes and roll up. Spread a thin film of sauce on bottom of greased baking dish and arrange crêpes in single layer in dish. Top with remaining sauce. Sprinkle with Swiss cheese. Dish can be refrigerated at this point. Before serving bake in 375° oven, uncovered, for 15 to 20 minutes or until hot, bubbly and lightly browned.

ENCHILADAS WITH CRÊPES
crêpes instead of tortillas—filled with chicken

12 wholewheat crêpes
2 tablespoons butter or margarine
1 cup chopped onion
1 clove garlic, minced
2 or 3 tablespoons chopped canned green chilis
1 cup tomato sauce
2-1/2 cups chopped cooked chicken
2 cups light cream
4 chicken bouillon cubes
1/2 lb. Jack cheese, shredded
avocado or green olives

In large skillet sauté onion and garlic in butter or margarine until tender. Add green chilis, tomato sauce and chicken. Stir well and simmer for 10 minutes. Divide mixture among crêpes, roll up and place in greased shallow baking dish, in single layer. Dish can be covered and refrigerated at this point. Heat cream and dissolve bouillon cubes in it. Before serving pour warmed cream mixture over crêpes. Top with shredded cheese and heat, uncovered, in 350° oven for 20 minutes or until hot and cheese has melted. Garnish with slices of avocado or sliced olives.

TURKEY CRÊPES
even leftovers can be festive this way

12 entrée crêpes
3 cups cubed cooked turkey
1 (10-3/4 oz.) can cream of chicken soup, undiluted
1-1/2 cups sour cream
1 teaspoon paprika
1 teaspoon salt
dill weed

Combine the cubed turkey, soup, 1/2 cup sour cream, paprika and salt. Stir to mix well. Divide the mixture among the crêpes and roll up. Place crêpes in single layer in greased shallow baking dish. Spread remaining sour cream over crêpes. Dish can be covered and refrigerated at this point. Before serving heat crêpes in 350° oven, uncovered, for 15 to 20 minutes or until hot and lightly browned. Garnish with a sprinkling of dill weed.

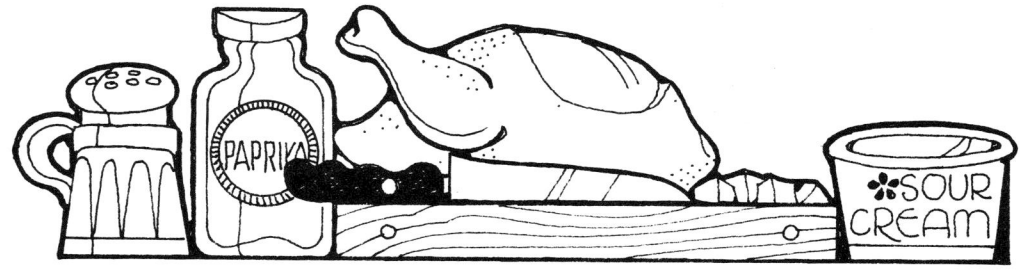

PORK AND SHRIMP CRÊPES
Filipino lumpia filling in crêpe wrapping

20 entrée crêpes
1/2 cup finely chopped onion
2 tablespoons butter or margarine
1/2 lb. cooked lean pork, cubed
1/2 lb. cooked shrimp meat
1 cup bean sprouts
2 cups shredded cabbage
5 medium carrots, shredded

1 cup raisins, soaked in water and drained
1 teaspoon garlic powder
4 tablespoons soy sauce
1 teaspoon salt
1/4 teaspoon pepper
1/3 cup vinegar
1 clove garlic, crushed

In a large skillet sauté onion in butter or margarine until transparent. Add pork, shrimp, bean sprouts, cabbage, carrots, raisins, garlic powder, 2 tablespoons soy sauce, salt and pepper. Stir to mix well and cook over medium heat for 5 minutes. Divide mixture among crêpes and fold into pockets. Place in greased shallow baking dish. Crêpes can be covered and refrigerated at this point. Before serving, uncover and bake in 400° oven for 20 minutes or until very hot and crispy. In the meantime, heat vinegar, 2 tablespoons soy sauce and crushed garlic in a small saucepan. Serve crêpes and let guest spoon hot vinegar sauce over each.

HUNGARIAN BEEF CRÊPES
try this delicious version of palascintas

12 entrée crêpes
6 slices bacon
2 lbs. boneless beef, cut into 1/2" cubes
1-1/2 cups chopped onion
1/2 lb. fresh mushrooms, washed and thinly sliced
3 cloves garlic, minced
1 tablespoon paprika
1 teaspoon salt

1/4 teaspoon pepper
1 (6 oz.) can tomato paste
2 cups water
4 beef bouillon cubes
1-1/2 cups dry red wine
2 teaspoons cornstarch
2 teaspoons water
sour cream

Cook bacon until crisp in frying pan. Remove from pan, cool and crumble; set aside. Brown beef cubes in drippings. Add onions, mushrooms, garlic and cook until onions are tender. Add paprika, salt, pepper, tomato paste, water, bouillon cubes and wine. Bring to boiling and simmer, uncovered, 1 hour. Blend cornstarch and water and stir into meat mixture. Cool, cover and chill for at least 2 hours or overnight. To assemble, divide filling among crêpes and roll. Place in single layer in greased shallow baking dish. Cover with foil and bake in 375° oven for about 20 to 25 minutes or until thoroughly heated. Garnish with sour cream and crumbled bacon.

MEXICAN STYLE CRÊPES
something different—burritos made with crêpes!

14 wholewheat crêpes
1 tablespoon cooking oil
1 lb. lean beef, cut into 1/2" cubes
1/2 lb. lean pork, cut into 1/2" cubes
1 cup chopped onion
3 cloves garlic, minced
1 teaspoon salt
1/2 teaspoon cumin
1-1/2 cups water
1 (4 oz.) can diced green chilis

1 tablespoon cornstarch
1 tablespoon cold water
1 tablespoon salad oil
1 (15-1/2 oz.) can refried beans
1 cup shredded sharp cheddar cheese
sour cream

In skillet over medium-high heat, cook beef and pork in 1 tablespoon oil until browned. Add onion, garlic, salt, cumin and water. Mix well and heat to boiling. Reduce heat to low, cover and simmer 2 hours or until meat is tender. Add chilis. Combine cornstarch and cold water. Add to meat mixture and stir until well thickened. In a 2-quart saucepan over medium heat, heat refried beans in 1 tablespoon hot oil. Add 1/2 cup cheese and stir until mixture is hot and cheese is melted. Divide and spread beans among crêpes. Top with meat mixture. Roll up and place in single layer in lightly greased shallow baking dish. Sprinkle with remaining 1/2 cup cheese. Cover and heat 10 to 15 minutes in 350° oven or until crêpes are hot. Serve with a spoonful of sour cream on each.

CANNELLONI
make the filling, sauce and crêpes ahead of time

16 entrée crêpes

Filling:
1 cup ricotta cheese or low-fat cottage cheese
1 egg beaten
1/3 cup shredded Parmesan cheese
1/4 teaspoon nutmeg
1 teaspoon salt
1/4 teaspoon pepper
1 (10 oz.) package frozen chopped spinach, thawed and squeezed free of liquid
1 (4 oz.) can chopped mushrooms, drained
1 lb. ground beef, browned and drained of fat

Sauce:
2 tablespoons olive oil
3/4 cup finely minced onion
1 stalk celery, finely minced
3 cloves garlic, finely minced
1 (16 oz.) can tomato sauce
1 (6 oz.) can tomato paste
2 cups dry red wine

1 teaspoon salt
1/2 teaspoon pepper
1/2 teaspoon sugar
1 teaspoon basil leaves

Topping:
1 (8 oz.) ball Mozzarella cheese, grated

To make filling, combine all ingredients and refrigerate until ready to assemble crêpes. To make sauce, sauté in large saucepan the onion, celery and garlic in oil until onion is tender. Add tomato sauce, tomato paste and wine. Mix well. Stir in salt, pepper, sugar and basil. Bring mixture to boil. Simmer over low heat for 1 to 2 hours, stirring occasionally. To assemble crêpes divide filling among crêpes and roll up. Spoon a thin film of sauce onto bottom of greased shallow baking dish and arrange crêpes in dish in single layer. Cover with remaining sauce and sprinkle with mozzerella cheese. Bake, uncovered, at 375° for 15 to 20 minutes or until hot and bubbly.

MANICOTTI WITH HAM AND CHEESE
an Italian favorite made the easy crêpe way

12 entrée crêpes
1/4 cup butter or margarine
1/4 cup all-purpose flour
2/3 cup milk
1 lb. diced fontina cheese
6 oz. diced teleme cheese
1/3 cup grated Parmesan cheese
2 tablespoons parsley flakes
12 thin slices cooked ham

In a saucepan melt butter or margarine. Stir in flour and cook until slightly browned, stirring constantly. Remove from heat and slowly pour in milk, stirring constantly. Return to heat and cook, stirring, until thick. Add fontina and teleme cheeses. Cook and stir until cheeses are melted. Remove from heat and add Parmesan cheese and parsley. To assemble manicotti, place a slice of ham on each crêpe. Divide filling among crêpes and roll up. Place in single layer in greased shallow baking dish. Cover with foil. Dish can be refrigerated at this point. Before serving bake, covered, in 375° oven for 15 to 20 minutes or until very hot. Uncover and bake 5 minutes longer or until slightly crisp.

ENGLISH "PORK PIE" CRÊPES
the same hearty filling but wrapped in a crêpe

14 beer crêpes
1-1/2 lbs. lean pork, cut into 1/2" cubes
1/2 cup finely minced onion
1-1/2 cups chicken broth
1 teaspoon sage
1/2 teaspoon mace
3/4 teaspoon salt
1/8 teaspoon pepper
1/2 (10 oz. size) package frozen peas and carrots
1/4 cup cold water
2 tablespoons cornstarch

In saucepan, brown pork and onion about 10 minutes. Stir in broth, sage, mace, salt and pepper. Cover tightly and simmer 1 hour or until meat is tender. Last 5 minutes of cooking add peas and carrots. Mix cold water and cornstarch and add to pork mixture, stirring constantly until very thick. Cool and divide evenly among crêpes. (Filling can be made a day or two ahead and refrigerated.) Fold into pockets and place in single layer in greased shallow baking dish. Cover and bake in 350° oven for 15 to 20 minutes or until hot.

ORIENTAL CRÊPES
let your guests assemble these great crêpes

18 entrée crêpes
1/2 lb. fresh bean sprouts

plum sauce:
1/3 cup plum jam
2/3 cup water
1 tablespoon soy sauce
1/4 teaspoon pepper
2 tablespoons vinegar
2 tablespoons cornstarch

fried egg strips:
3 eggs
3 tablespoons water
1/4 teaspoon salt

pork filling:
2 tablespoons soy sauce
2 tablespoons water
1 tablespoon cornstarch
2 tablespoons cooking oil
3 cloves garlic, minced
1/4 lb. fresh mushrooms, sliced
1/2 cup minced onion
1 lb. lean, boneless pork, cut into thin 1-1/2 inch strips
1/4 lb. crab meat
1 cup salted, chopped, roasted peanuts

Place bean sprouts in colander. Pour 2 quarts boiling water over them; drain. Bean sprouts may be covered and refrigerated at this point. Serve at room temperature.

In saucepan combine plum jam, water, soy sauce and pepper. Cook over medium heat, stirring, until jam melts. Mix together vinegar and cornstarch. Add to plum mixture and cook, stirring, until it thickens. Plum sauce can be covered and refrigerated at this point. Serve at room temperature.

Beat together eggs, water and salt. Place a 6 or 7 inch frying pan over medium heat. When hot, remove from heat and pour 1 tablespoon cooking oil into bottom of pan. Pour 3 tablespoons of egg mixture into pan, tilting to spread evenly. Set pan back on heat and cook until egg is set. Slide egg out of pan with a spatula and cool on paper towel. Repeat procedure to make about 6. Stack and cut into thin strips. Egg strips can be covered and refrigerated at this point. Serve at room temperature.

Combine soy sauce, water and cornstarch; set aside. Pour 1 tablespoon cooking oil into wok or large frying pan and place over high heat. Add garlic and stir-fry until golden brown. Add mushrooms and stir-fry 1 minute. Remove to a bowl. Add another tablespoon of cooking oil and add onion; stir-fry until tender. Add pork and stir-fry for 4 minutes. Add mushrooms and crabmeat. Toss to mix well. Add cornstarch mixture and cook until thickened. Serve hot.

To assemble, spread each crêpe with 1 tablespoon plum sauce. Add a sprinkling of bean sprouts, egg strips, 3 or 4 tablespoons pork filling and a spoonful of peanuts. Roll up crêpes. A great idea for a buffet supper.

BREAKFAST CRÊPES
make these the night before and you're ready for guests

16 entrée crêpes
1/4 lb. bulk pork sausage
3/4 cup chopped onion
2 cloves garlic, minced
1 (10 oz.) package frozen chopped spinach,
   thawed and squeezed free of all liquid
1 egg, beaten
1 cup small curd cottage cheese
1/4 cup Parmesan cheese

1 tablespoon parsley flakes
1 teaspoon salt
1/2 teaspoon thyme
1/2 teaspoon marjoram
1/4 cup butter or margarine
1 (28 oz.) can tomatoes, drained well and chopped
1/2 teaspoon basil
1/2 teaspoon salt
1/4 teaspoon pepper

Brown sausage in skillet. Remove and drain well. In sausage drippings sauté onion and garlic until limp. Remove from skillet and drain. Combine sausage, onion, garlic, spinach, egg, cottage cheese, Parmesan cheese, parsley, salt, thyme and marjoram. Mix well. Divide evenly among crêpes and roll up. Place in single layer in greased shallow baking dish. Dish can be covered and refrigerated at this point. Before serving make sauce by combining butter or margarine, tomatoes, basil, salt and pepper in saucepan and bringing to a boil. Simmer for 10 minutes. Pour sauce over filled crêpes and bake, uncovered, in 350° oven 15 to 20 minutes or until hot.

LAMB CURRY CRÊPES
leftover lamb? wrap it up with India's spices

12 entrée crêpes
1-1/2 cups cubed lean cooked lamb
2 cups chopped onion
2 cups chopped unpeeled apples
1/4 cup butter or margarine
1-1/2 tablespoons curry powder
1 teaspoon ground ginger

1 teaspoon chili powder
1/2 teaspoon pepper
1 tablespoon catsup
1 cup chicken broth
1 tablespoon cornstarch
1 tablespoon water
chutney

Melt butter or margarine in large skillet. Sauté onions and apples until tender. Sprinkle with curry, ginger, chili powder and pepper. Add catsup and stir well. Add broth and cover pan; simmer gently for 20 minutes. Combine cornstarch and water and add to mixture, stirring until thickened. Add lamb. Stir to mix well. Simmer, uncovered, for 20 minutes. Divide mixture evenly among crêpes and roll up. Place in single layer in greased shallow baking dish. Dish may be covered and refrigerated at this point. Before serving cover crêpes and heat in 350° oven for 15 to 20 minutes or until hot. Serve with chutney.

SHRIMP AND MUSHROOM CRÊPES
a tasty combination topped with cheese

16 entrée crêpes
6 tablespoons butter or margarine
1/4 cup chopped shallots or green onions
1/2 lb. fresh mushrooms, chopped
1 teaspoon tarragon leaves
1/4 cup all-purpose flour
2 cups chicken broth
1 cup evaporated milk

1 teaspoon salt
1/4 teaspoon pepper
1 teaspoon lemon juice
1 lb. cooked, tiny shrimp
1/2 cup grated Parmesan cheese
1/2 cup Swiss cheese
3 tablespoons butter or margarine

In skillet melt 2 tablespoons butter or margarine and sauté shallots or green onions and mushrooms until they are limp. Stir in tarragon leaves; set aside. In saucepan melt 4 tablespoons butter or margarine. Add flour and cook, stirring constantly over low heat, for 1 minute. Gradually add broth and milk. Cook, stirring constantly, over medium heat until it comes to a boil. Boil slowly for 15 seconds. Remove from heat at once and add salt, pepper and lemon juice. Combine shrimp, mushroom mixture and 3/4 cup of sauce; mix well. Divide filling evenly among crêpes and roll up. Spread a thin film of sauce on bottom of greased shallow baking dish. Arrange crêpes in dish in a single layer. Top with remaining sauce. Sprinkle the two cheeses over the sauce. Dot with butter or margarine. Dish can be covered and refrigerated at this point. Before serving bake in 375° oven, uncovered, for 15 to 20 minutes or until hot, bubbly and lightly browned.

SHRIMP-FILLED CRÊPES
a touch of dill weed adds a nice zest

12 entrée crêpes
1 cup sour cream
1 tablespoon dill weed
1 teaspoon salt
1/4 teaspoon pepper
1 lb. cooked shrimp
2 cups grated Swiss cheese
2 tablespoons butter

Spread each crêpe with a tablespoon of sour cream mixed with dill weed, salt and pepper. Divide shrimp evenly among crêpes. Roll or fold each crêpe and place in single layer in greased shallow baking dish. Top with grated cheese and dot with butter. Dish may be covered and refrigerated at this point. Before serving bake, uncovered, in 350° oven until very hot and lightly browned.

CRAB CRÊPES
garnished with avocado slices and sour cream

12 entrée crêpes
1 lb. fresh crab meat
1-1/2 cups sour cream

1/2 cup shredded Parmesan cheese
2 avocados, peeled and sliced
2 tablespoons lemon juice

Combine crab meat and 3/4 cup sour cream; mix well. Divide mixture evenly among crêpes. Roll up and place in single layer in greased shallow baking dish. Sprinkle with Parmesan cheese. Dish can be covered and refrigerated at this point. Before serving bake, covered, in 400° oven for 20 minutes. Remove from oven and garnish crêpes with remaining sour cream and avocado slices which have been dipped in lemon juice.

GREAT TUNA CRÊPES
a family version of Russian blinchiki

8 entrée crêpes
1 (6-1/2 oz.) can chunk style tuna, well drained
1/3 cup thinly sliced green onion
1/3 cup minced celery
1/3 cup chopped black olives
1/3 cup chopped salted, dry roasted peanuts
1/3 cup sour cream
1 teaspoon lemon juice
3/4 teaspoon dill weed
sour cream

Combine tuna, onion, celery, black olives, peanuts, sour cream, lemon juice and dill weed, mixing well. Divide filling evenly among crêpes. Fold in pocket fashion and place seam side down in single layer in greased shallow baking dish. Dish can be covered and refrigerated at this point. Before serving bake, covered, in 350° oven for 15 to 20 minutes. Serve immediately with a dollop of sour cream on each if you wish.

BROCCOLI AND CHEESE CRÊPES
a delicious choice for luncheon

16 entrée crêpes
filling:
2 (10 oz.) packages frozen chopped broccoli
2 tablespoons butter or margarine
2 tablespoons chopped onion
1 (6 oz.) can chopped mushrooms, drained
2 tablespoons flour
1/2 cup light cream
1/4 cup chicken broth
2 tablespoons grated Parmesan cheese
1 (4 oz.) can water chestnuts, drained and chopped
1 teaspoon salt
1/8 teaspoon pepper
sauce:
1/2 cup butter or margarine
1/2 cup flour
1-1/2 cups light cream
2 cups milk
1-1/2 cups grated Parmesan cheese
2 teaspoons prepared mustard
1 teaspoon salt

Cook the broccoli according to package directions and drain well; set aside. In large skillet melt butter or margarine and sauté onions and mushrooms until lightly browned. Stir in flour. Add cream and chicken broth. Cook, stirring, until thickened. Add 2 tablespoons grated cheese, water chestnuts, salt, pepper and broccoli. Set aside. To make sauce, melt butter and stir in flour. Add cream and milk and stir until well blended. Add Parmesan cheese, mustard and salt and stir until thickened and cheese has melted. Set aside. Divide filling among crêpes and fold or roll up. Place crêpes in single layer in greased shallow baking dish. Pour sauce over all. Dish can be covered and refrigerated at this point. Before serving bake, uncovered, in 350° oven for 25 to 30 minutes or until bubbly and lightly browned.

CHEESE BLINTZES

a brunch favorite—topped with sour cream and jam

12 sour cream crêpes
2 cups (1 lb.) ricotta cheese or low-fat cottage cheese
1 egg yolk
1 teaspoon salt
1 tablespoon melted butter or margarine
2 tablespoons sugar (optional)
1 teaspoon lemon juice (optional)
sour cream
strawberry jam

Beat cheese, egg yolk, salt and butter or margarine together. Add sugar or lemon juice as you prefer. Divide evenly among crêpes and fold into pockets. (Spoon mixture on browned side of crêpe.) Place seam-side down in a single layer in a greased shallow baking dish. Dish can be covered and refrigerated at this point. Before serving uncover and heat in 350° oven for 10 to 15 minutes or until hot. Serve with sour cream and strawberry jam for topping.

40

EASY CHILI RELLENOS
a simple way to make this zesty Mexican treat

12 entrée crêpes
2 (4 oz.) cans mild whole chili peppers
1/2 lb. sharp Cheddar cheese

Cut chili peppers into halves and wash to remove all seeds. Cut cheese into domino size pieces. Wrap each piece of cheese in a chili half and place on crêpe. Fold crêpes into pockets and place seam-side down in a single layer in greased shallow baking dish. Dish can be covered and refrigerated at this point. Before serving bake, covered, in 350° oven for 15 to 20 minutes or until hot and cheese has melted.

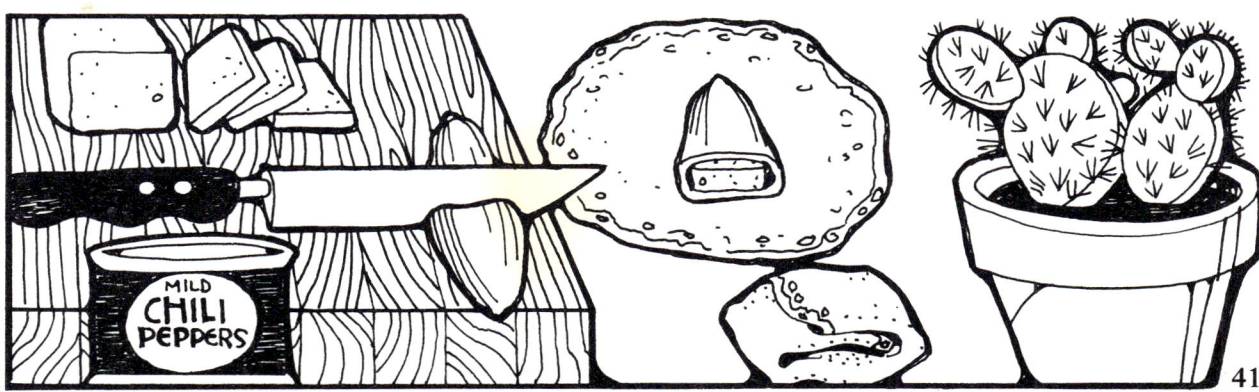

VEGETABLE BLINTZES
filled with cabbage, carrots, peppers and onions

12 sour cream crêpes
1 cup shredded cabbage
1 cup grated carrots
1/2 cup finely sliced green pepper
1 cup diced onion
3 tablespoons butter or margarine
1 teaspoon salt
1/8 teaspoon cayenne
sour cream

Combine the cabbage, carrots, green pepper and onion and sauté in butter or margarine in a large skillet for 10 minutes. Season with salt and cayenne. Divide filling evenly among crêpes and fold into pockets. (Spoon mixture on browned side of crêpe.) Place seam-side down in single layer in greased shallow baking dish. Dish can be covered and refrigerated at this point. Before serving bake, uncovered, in 350° oven for 15 to 20 minutes or until hot. Serve with sour cream for topping.

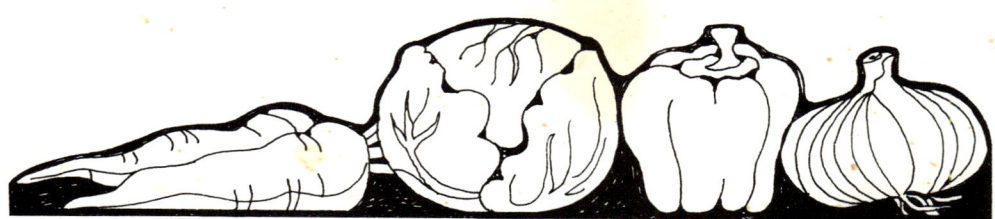

MUSHROOM CRÊPES
add a salad and dessert for a great luncheon

12 entrée crêpes
1/2 cup butter or margarine
1 lb. fresh mushrooms, sliced
1/2 cup thinly sliced green onion
1 teaspoon basil leaves
1/4 cup all-purpose flour
1-1/2 cups chicken broth
1/2 cup dry white wine
1 cup heavy cream
1 teaspoon salt
1/2 teaspoon pepper
1 cup grated Swiss cheese

Melt 1/4 cup butter or margarine in large skillet. Sauté green onions and mushrooms until limp. Stir in basil leaves; set aside. In saucepan melt remaining butter or margarine. Add flour and cook until foamy. Gradually add broth, wine, and cream. Stir constantly over medium heat until at boiling point. Boil gently until mixture thickens. Remove from heat and add salt and pepper. Combine mushroom mixture and 2/3 cup of sauce, mixing well. Divide filling evenly among crêpes and roll up. Spread a thin film of sauce on bottom of greased baking dish. Arrange crêpes in a single layer in dish. Top with remainder of sauce. Sprinkle with cheese. Dish can be refrigerated at this point. Before serving bake, uncovered, in 375° oven for 15 to 20 minutes or until sauce is bubbly. Place dish under broiler for a few minutes to lightly brown the crêpes and sauce.

MANICOTTI WITH SPINACH AND CHEESE
a meatless dish that's packed with protein

12 entrée crêpes
2 (10 oz.) packages frozen chopped spinach, thawed and squeezed free of all liquid
1 teaspoon salt
1/4 teaspoon pepper
1/2 teaspoon garlic powder
1/2 teaspoon onion powder
1/2 teaspoon nutmeg
2 cups (1 lb.) ricotta cheese or low-fat cottage cheese
2 eggs
2-1/2 cups shredded Jack cheese
1/2 cup grated Parmesan cheese

Put spinach in mixing bowl with salt, pepper, garlic powder, onion powder, nutmeg, ricotta or cottage cheese, eggs, 1-1/2 cups Jack cheese and Parmesan cheese. Stir to mix well. Divide mixture evenly among crêpes and roll up. Place crêpes in a single layer in greased shallow baking dish. Cover with foil. Dish can be refrigerated at this point. Before serving bake in 375° oven for 15 to 20 minutes or until thoroughly heated. Remove foil and sprinkle with remaining shredded Jack cheese. Bake, uncovered, 5 minutes more or until cheese has melted.

ZUCCHINI CRÊPES
try this tempting way with zucchini

12 entrée crêpes
1 cup dry bread crumbs
1/2 cup butter or margarine
1/4 cup minced onion

2 cups shredded zucchini
3 eggs, beaten
3 tablespoons parsley flakes
1/2 cup Parmesan cheese

In a large skillet sauté bread crumbs in 1/4 cup butter or margarine until toasted; set aside. Add remaining butter or margarine to pan and sauté minced onion and shredded zucchini until both are tender and lightly browned. Add beaten eggs and scramble over low heat. Combine eggs with bread crumbs and parsley and mix well. Divide the mixture among crêpes and fold or roll up. Arrange crêpes in a single layer in greased shallow baking dish. Sprinkle with Parmesan cheese. Dish can be covered and refrigerated at this point. Before serving heat, uncovered, in 375° oven for 10 minutes or until crêpes are hot and cheese has melted.

RATATOUILLE CRÊPES
a great mix of eggplant, zucchini, green peppers and tomatoes

16 entrée crêpes
1/3 cup cooking oil
2 cloves garlic, minced
1 large onion, sliced
3 tablespoons flour
1 (1 lb.) eggplant, diced
2 zucchini, thinly sliced

2 green peppers, seeded and cut into thin strips
1 (29-oz.) can Italian-style tomatoes
1 teaspoon salt
1/4 teaspoon pepper
1 tablespoon capers (optional)
1 cup grated Swiss cheese

Heat oil in a large skillet. Add garlic and onion and sauté until onion is transparent. Meanwhile lightly flour the diced eggplant and sliced zucchini. Add the zucchini, eggplant and green pepper to onion and garlic. Stir to mix well and cook, uncovered, for 10 minutes. Add tomatoes, salt and pepper, and cook, covered, for 30 minutes. Uncover and cook for 30 minutes longer or until mixture is thick. Add capers during last 15 minutes of cooking. Divide the mixture evenly among crêpes and roll up or fold. Place in single layer in greased shallow baking dish. Top with grated Swiss cheese. Dish can be covered and refrigerated at this point. Before serving bake, uncovered, in 350° oven for 20 minutes or until hot and cheese has melted.

SERVE A DAZZLING DESSERT

CHERRIES JUBILEE CRÊPES
a gorgeous dessert topped with whipped cream

16 dessert crêpes
2 (1 lb.) cans pitted dark sweet cherries
1/4 cup cornstarch
1 (10 oz.) jar red currant jelly
1 pint vanilla ice cream
whipped cream

Drain juice from cherries and reserve. Add cornstarch to juice and set aside. In saucepan over low heat melt jelly. Add cornstarch-juice mixture and cook until thick. Add cherries to sauce and heat well. Place about 2 tablespoons of ice cream on each crêpe, roll up and place crêpes on individual serving plates. Spoon cherries and sauce over all and top with a dollop of whipped cream.

CRÊPES IN BRANDIED APRICOT SAUCE
very, very easy and very, very good

16 orange-honey dessert crêpes
1 (12 oz.) can apricot nectar
1 tablespoon grated orange peel
3 tablespoons butter
1/4 cup sugar
1/4 cup brandy, warmed

Combine and heat in a small saucepan the nectar, orange peel and butter. Fold crêpes into wedges and arrange in a shallow serving dish. Pour hot sauce over crêpes. Sprinkle with sugar. Pour warmed brandy over all and flame. Spoon sauce over the crêpes until the flaming stops. Serve immediately.

CRÊPES SUZETTE
an easy version of this famous dessert

12 dessert crêpes
4 lumps sugar
1 orange
1/2 cup butter
1/4 cup orange liqueur
1/4 cup cognac or brandy, warmed

Rub the lumps of sugar on the orange skin to absorb the aromatic oil. Squeeze the orange and reserve the juice. Crush the orange-sugar with 1/4 cup butter and cream well. Place remaining 1/4 cup butter in skillet or chafing dish and melt over low heat. Add orange butter, orange juice, and orange liqueur; stir until well blended. Keep the sauce at a low simmer. Use a serving spoon and fork to dip each crêpe into the sauce and fold into wedges, arranging attractively in skillet or chafing dish. Pour warmed brandy or cognac over all and flame. Spoon the liqueur over the crêpes until flaming stops. Serve immediately.

ROYAL BANANA CRÊPES
an impressive dessert that's so easy

16 dessert crêpes
1/2 cup butter or margarine
1/2 cup firmly packed brown sugar
1/2 teaspoon cinnamon
1/2 teaspoon nutmeg
4 large bananas, peeled
1/2 cup light cream
whipped cream

In a heavy saucepan melt butter or margarine. Stir in brown sugar, cinnamon and nutmeg. Cut bananas in half, then cut in half lengthwise. Add bananas to sauce and spoon sauce over to coat them well. Stir in cream, cooking until slightly thickened. Remove from heat. Roll each piece of banana in a crêpe. Place seam-side down in a single layer in greased shallow baking dish. Heat in 350° oven for 8 minutes or until hot. Serve with warmed sauce from bananas and whipped cream.

PEACHY APPLE CRÊPES
make these early and heat just before serving

12 dessert crêpes
1 cup raisins, soaked in 1/4 cup brandy
1 cup peach jam
1-1/2 cups finely diced peeled apples
3 tablespoons melted butter or margarine
3 tablespoons sugar

Soak raisins in brandy for 15 minutes; drain and reserve liquid. Combine peach jam, apples and raisins. Divide evenly among crêpes and roll up or fold into wedges. Place crêpes in greased shallow baking dish in single layer. Brush with melted butter or margarine and sprinkle with sugar. Dish can be covered and refrigerated at this point. Before serving heat, uncovered, in 350° oven for 15 minutes or until very hot. Warm the reserved brandy and pour over hot crêpes. Flame if desired. Spoon brandy over crêpes until flaming stops.

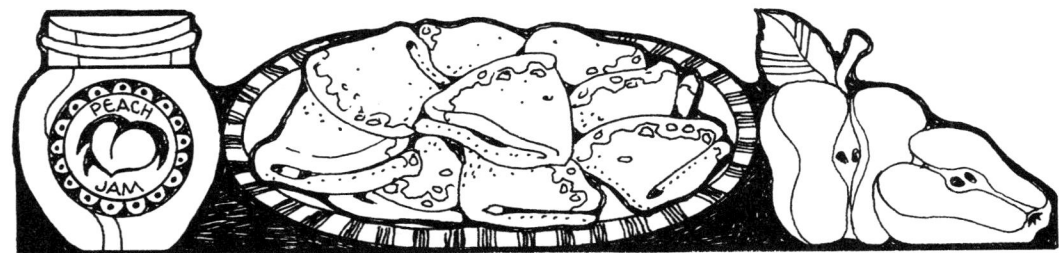

STRAWBERRY CHANTILLY CRÊPES
a wrap-up of strawberries and whipped cream

12 dessert crêpes
3 cups hulled and halved strawberries
1/4 cup granulated sugar
1 cup whipping cream
2 tablespoons kirsch
whole strawberries for garnish

Ten minutes before serving add sugar to prepared strawberries and mix well. Whip cream and add kirsch. Gently fold strawberries into whipped cream-kirsch mixture. Divide filling among crêpes, reserving 1 cup of filling for garnish. Roll up or fold crêpes into wedges and top each with a spoonful of reserved filling and garnish with whole strawberries.

RASPBERRY SUPREME CRÊPES
a delicious sauce over orange crêpes

18 orange-honey dessert crêpes
2 (10 oz.) packages frozen raspberries, thawed
2 tablespoons sugar
2 tablespoons cornstarch
1/4 cup cold water
1 tablespoon cognac or brandy (optional)
whipped cream

Mix raspberries with sugar in saucepan and heat to a boil, stirring constantly. Mix cornstarch with cold water and add to raspberries. Cook until thickened, stirring frequently. Add cognac or brandy. Fold crêpes into wedges and arrange on serving plates. Spoon warm raspberry sauce over crêpes. Top with whipped cream.

PINEAPPLE-COCONUT CRÊPES
a perfect complement of flavors and textures

8 dessert crêpes
2 cups crushed pineapple, well drained
1 cup grated coconut
1/4 cup dark rum
1/4 cup melted butter or margarine
1/3 cup sugar

Combine pineapple, coconut and rum. Divide mixture evenly among crêpes. Roll up or fold and place in single layer in greased shallow baking dish. Brush with melted butter or margarine and sprinkle with sugar. Dish may be covered and refrigerated at this point. Before serving uncover and heat crêpes in 350° oven for 15 to 20 minutes or until very hot and sugar begins to carmelize. If you wish, warm 1/4 cup additional rum and pour over crêpes and flame. Spoon liquid over crêpes until flaming stops.

FRESH PEACH CRÊPES
orange juice and liqueur make these special

16 orange honey dessert crêpes
3 cups peeled and sliced fresh peaches
1/4 cup orange juice
1/4 cup plus 1 tablespoon orange liqueur
1/2 cup sugar
1 cup whipping cream
2 tablespoons sugar

Ten minutes before serving add orange juice, 1/4 cup orange liqueur and sugar to peaches; set aside. Whip cream and flavor with 1 tablespoon orange liqueur and 2 tablespoons sugar. Divide peaches among crêpes and roll up or fold into wedges. Top crêpe with a generous spoonful of flavored whipped cream.

COFFEE CRÊPES
coffee-cream filling topped with coffee sauce

16 dessert crêpes
1 cup sugar
6 egg yolks
1/2 cup all-purpose flour
1 tablespoon instant coffee powder
2 cups milk, scalded

2 teaspoons butter
1 teaspoon vanilla extract
1 cup firmly packed brown sugar
1 cup strong coffee
1/2 teaspoon vanilla
1 tablespoon brandy

In a saucepan, beat the sugar into the egg yolks with a wire whisk and continue to whip until light. Beat in flour until well blended. Stir instant coffee into hot milk and add to eggs whisking constantly until smooth. Over medium heat, cook and stir constantly until thick and custardy. Remove from heat and beat in butter and vanilla extract. Continue whisking a few minutes and let cool. Divide filling among crêpes and roll up. Place in a single layer in greased shallow baking dish. Dish can be covered and refrigerated at this point. Before serving heat in 350° oven for 8 to 10 minutes or until hot. In the meantime combine brown sugar and coffee in a saucepan and bring to a boil. Boil uncovered for 8 to 10 minutes. Remove from heat and add vanilla and brandy. Pour over hot filled crêpes.

PINEAPPLE CREAM CRÊPES
a perfect ending to a special dinner

10 dessert crêpes
1 (8-1/4 oz.) can crushed pineapple
2-1/2 cups milk
3/4 cup sugar
1/2 teaspoon salt
1/4 cup cornstarch
3 egg yolks, lightly beaten
1 teaspoon vanilla

Drain crushed pineapple, reserving liquid and set aside. In a saucepan scald the milk and add sugar and salt. Stir to mix well. Mix pineapple liquid and cornstarch and add to milk mixture. Cook over low heat until mixture thickens. Cover and cook 10 minutes. Add a few tablespoons of the hot mixture to the egg yolks, a little at a time, stirring constantly. Add yolk mixture to the hot mixture and cook over very low heat, stirring constantly, until thickened. Cool this cream filling and add vanilla. Filling can be refrigerated for a few hours at this point. Before serving divide the filling among the crêpes and roll. Arrange crêpes on individual serving plates and garnish each with a spoonful of crushed pineapple.

ORANGE HONEY SAUCED CRÊPES
a delicious confection that rates applause

16 orange honey dessert crêpes
1/3 cup honey
3 tablespoons butter or margarine
3/4 teaspoon cinnamon
2 teaspoons grated orange peel
1 (6 oz.) can frozen orange juice concentrate, thawed
1 cup orange juice
whipped cream

Combine honey, butter or margarine, cinnamon, orange peel, orange juice concentrate and orange juice in saucepan. Bring to boil and gently boil for 5 minutes, stirring occasionally. Fold crêpes into wedges and arrange attractively on serving plates. Pour hot sauce over crêpes and serve with a generous spoonful of whipped cream.

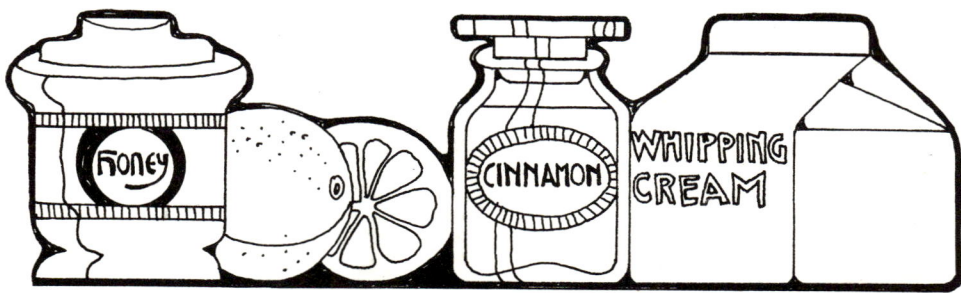

APPLE BLINTZES
add this to your apple repertoire

16 sour cream crêpes
1 egg white
2 cups finely chopped, peeled apples
5 tablespoons sugar
1 teaspoon cinnamon
1/4 cup brown sugar, firmly packed
3 tablespoons melted butter or margarine

Beat the egg white until it begins to stiffen. Fold in the apples, sugar and cinnamon. Divide the filling evenly among the crêpes and fold crêpes into pockets. (Spoon mixture onto browned side of crêpe.) Arrange seam-side down in a single layer in greased shallow baking dish. Sprinkle with brown sugar and drizzle with melted butter or margarine. Bake in 400° oven for 15 minutes or until hot.

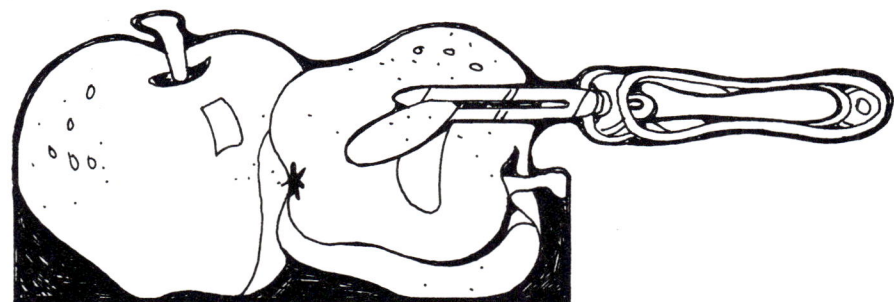

APRICOT CREAM CRÊPES
cream-filled crêpes with a hot apricot sauce

12 dessert crêpes
1 (16 oz.) can apricots, drained
1 (3 oz.) package cream cheese, softened
1/4 cup confectioners' sugar
1 cup whipping cream
1 tablespoon apricot brandy
1 (12 oz.) can apricot nectar
4 teaspoons cornstarch
4 teaspoons cold water

Cut apricots into tiny pieces and drain again. In a small bowl with mixer at medium speed, beat cream cheese and confectioners' sugar until smooth. Slowly beat in whipping cream until mixture is smooth and thick. Fold in apricot brandy and apricot pieces. Divide mixture evenly among crêpes. Roll up and set aside. Crêpes can be covered and refrigerated at this point. Before serving bring apricot nectar to boiling point in a saucepan over medium heat. Stir in cornstarch mixed with water. Cook until thickened. Serve hot sauce over crêpes.

MERINGUE CHERRY CRÊPES
be a wizard of "ahs" with this dessert

8 dessert crêpes
1 (16-oz.) can tart red pitted cherries, undrained
1/2 cup sugar
1/2 teaspoon cinnamon
1 tablespoon cornstarch
1 tablespoon cold water
3 egg whites
1/3 cup sugar
1/4 cup finely chopped almonds

In saucepan combine cherries, their liquid, sugar and cinnamon. Bring mixture to boiling point. Stir in cornstarch combined with water. Cook over low heat, stirring constantly, until mixture thickens. Remove from heat and cool 15 minutes. Then remove cherries with slotted spoon, reserving the sauce. Divide the cherries evenly among crêpes and roll up. Pour sauce in shallow baking dish and arrange filled crêpes on top. Beat egg whites until frothy. Gradually sprinkle sugar over top, beating until stiff peaks form. Fold in almonds. Spread meringue over crêpes in decorative fashion. Bake at 425° for several minutes or until meringue is lightly browned. Serve warm.

HOT FUDGE CRÊPES
an all-time favorite turned out with new elegance

8 dessert crêpes
1/4 cup butter or margarine
2 (1 oz.) squares unsweetened chocolate
1/2 cup granulated sugar
1/8 teaspoon salt
1/2 cup evaporated milk
1 pint vanilla or chocolate ice cream

In saucepan, melt butter or margarine and chocolate. Gradually add sugar and salt. Stir in milk and cook until smooth, stirring constantly. Divide ice cream among crêpes by placing generous spoonfuls on each. Roll up and place on serving plates. Top each with hot fudge sauce. (A dollop of whipped cream and a cherry add to the fun.)

PEAR CRÊPES DELUXE
put these together with ingredients on hand

12 dessert crêpes
1 (1 lb. 13 oz.) can pear halves, drained
3/4 cup maple syrup
1/4 cup lemon juice
cinnamon

Slice pear halves into quarters and cook in a saucepan with syrup and lemon juice for about 3 minutes or until pear slices are thoroughly heated. Divide pears among crêpes and roll up. Place crêpes on serving plates and spoon heated syrup over each. Add a sprinkling of cinnamon. (For variety, fill crêpes with vanilla ice cream, roll up and spoon warm pears and syrup over all.)

RECIPE INDEX

Typography by TAPESET of San Francisco.
Printing by Consolidated Printers, Inc., of Berkeley